Eutrophication: The Death of a Water body

Dr. Hemant Pathak

ISBN: 148417142X
ISBN-13: 978-1484171424

DEDICATION

Dedicated to Shri Sainath Maharaj the all omnipotent of world the most merciful.

CONTENTS

Foreword

Eutrophication: The Death of a Water body; provides a unique insight into the problems our planet faces in terms of water quality and quantity, and what to do about it. This is the only books expressed comprehensive and interdisciplinary focus to hydrological understanding with the multidimensional approach.

This book made of 07 years consistently research on water resources, makes it ideal source for students, teachers, industrialist, water experts and environmentalists.

This book provides an essential guide to researchers, it offers: various aspects of water; on the challenges and experiences in present scenario.

Simply explained, Water Pollution is an important book for all who wish to make a difference in how to plan and manage our water resources.

Until and unless Water, that magical substance from which all life springs forth, is essential to the very existence of every life form on earth. The role of water in the living organism has not changed since life's first creation in salt water billions of years ago.

Dr. Hemant Pathak

M.Sc. (Gold medalist), Ph. D.

Assistant Professor of Engineering Chemistry

Indira Gandhi Govt. Engineering College,

Sagar, MP, India

Glossary

anoxic conditions	No oxygen present
Biomanipulation	Change in biological structure by removing and/or stocking living organisms
Chlorophyll a	Green pigment in plants that promotes photosynthesis
Eutrophication	Nutrient rich
External loading	Nutrients from outside the lake, for instance nutrients in wastewater discharge to the lake, or nutrients from agricultural drainage water
Internal loading	Nutrients from the lake itself, for instance release of nutrients or toxic substances from the sediment (the muddy bottom layer) of the lake
Sediment	Bottom and muddy layer of a lake
Photosynthesis	Formation of plant biomass from nutrients with solar radiation as the energy source
Phytoplankton	Free-floating microscopic plants
Point pollution	Polluted water from a defined point. It can be collected as industrial or municipal wastewater
Non-point pollution	Pollution mainly from agriculture or dumping grounds

EUTROPHICATION: THE DEATH OF A WATER BODY

1. Introduction

How can we conserve our lakes and reservoirs from eutrophication with a growing population, growing urbanization and growing industrial production? That is an enormous challenge.

The present book entitled "Eutrophication: The Death of a Water body" provides an overview of the problem of the enrichment of surface freshwater bodies due to organic compounds originating from urban and agricultural activities as well as from industrial effluents. Eutrophication is a process in water bodies that once started is difficult to control unless immediate action is taken and it will ultimately reduce oxygen in water killing fish and other organisms, reduce biodiversity and cause enormous economic losses.

Water eutrophication is mainly caused by excessive loading of nutrients into water bodies like N and P. Excessive nutrients come from both point pollution such as waste water from industry and municipal sewage, and non-point pollution like irrigation water, surface run water containing fertilizer from farmland, etc.

Lakes and estuaries accumulating large amounts of plant nutrients are called "eutrophic" (from the Greek words *eu* meaning "well" and *trophe* meaning "nourishment"). Water eutrophication has become a worldwide environmental problem in recent years, and understanding the water eutrophication will help for prevention and remediation of water resources from this world-wide problems.

Water eutrophication in lakes, estuaries, reservoirs and rivers is widespread all over the world and the severity is increasing day by day. The major influencing factors on water eutrophication include nutrient enrichment, hydrodynamics, environmental factors such as temperature, salinity, carbon dioxide, element balance, etc., and microbial and biodiversity.

The occurrence of water eutrophication is actually a complex function of all the possible influencing factors. By proper environmental and ecologically sound planning, it is possible to avoid eutrophication, and other pollution problems, but it requires urgent action now not later.

2. What is Eutrophication ?

Eutrophication is a process in which a water body, such as a lake, becomes rich of nutrients (phosphorus, nitrogen etc.) from domestic drainage as well as water runoff from agricultural fields. Increasing nutrients cause a change of the nutritional status of a body of water thus enrichment of biological productivity. But this deteriorated water quality inadequate for domestic, recreational and other uses. This process accelerated by enrichment of nutritive metals in the water bodies is a result of precipitation, ground water inflow, contiguous drainage basin and by human activities that increase the rate of nutrient input in a water body, due to rapid urbanization, industrialization and intensifying agricultural production. For lake aquatic ecosystems, human activities in the watershed can lead to loss of dominant species and functional groups, high nutrient turnover, low resistance, high porosity of nutrients and sediments, and the loss of productivity. The plants and sediments accumulate gradually, and eventually destroy the water bodies.

Eutrophic ponds have such high material deposition that a variety of nutrients are released into the water, which support large populations of algae and higher plants. Nitrogen and phosphorus become the main constituents of the water which originate from household detergents and municipal and industrial waste water.

The influence of the human activities, excessive nitrogen, phosphorus and other nutrients are loaded into water bodies like lake, reservoirs etc could cause negative ecological consequences on aquatic ecosystem structures, processes and functions, result in the fast growth of algae and other plankton, and deteriorate water quality.

These nutrients resulting in increased production of algae and macrophytes. This enhanced plant growth (algal bloom), reduces dissolved oxygen in the water when dead plant material decomposes and can cause other organisms to die. Due to excessive growth of macrophytes in water and algae floating on the water surface, the photosynthesis process of aquatic flora decreases leading to decreased production of oxygen in the water body. This excessive growth also decreases the oxygen transfer from air to water by diffusion.

Enrichment of aquatic systems by addition of fertilizers into lakes is subject to adverse impacts. Phosphorus is often regarded as the main culprit in cases of eutrophication in lakes subjected to point source pollution from sewage.

Urban sewages, agriculture runoff and pollution from septic systems and, and other human-related activities increase the flux of both inorganic nutrients and organic substances water. Elevated atmospheric compounds of nitrogen can increase soil nitrogen availability.

When algae and zooplankton die and sink to the bottom of the water body, their decay by bacteria reduces the concentration of dissolved oxygen in the bottom of water body further to levels which may not be sufficient to support fish life.

The bilinear interactions of variables such as the cumulative concentration of nutrients, densities of algae (phytoplankton) and zooplankton populations, density of detritus and concentration of dissolved oxygen are considered. We consider that various nutrients are supplied to the water body from domestic drainage as well as run off from agricultural fields. These nutrients may also be supplied by death of algae and zooplankton. Lakes and reservoirs can be classified according to the extent of their eutrophication (or nutrients enrichment) into four main classes: oligotrophic, mesotrophic, eutrophic and hypereutrophic.

It is based on concentrations of phosphorus, nitrogen and chlorophyll a (green plant pigment needed in photosynthesis).

Eutrophication is frequently a result of nutrient pollution such as the release of sewage effluent into natural waters, a low concentration of dissolved oxygen. Following adverse ecological effects of eutrophication increased biomass of phytoplankton.

• Toxic or inedible phytoplankton species

• Decreases in water transparency

• Taste, odor problems

• Dissolved oxygen depletion

• Increased incidences of fish kills

• Loss of desirable fish species

• Decreases in perceived aesthetic value of the water body

At certain pH levels, higher NH3 are toxic to aquatic life, therefore detrimental to the ecological balance of water bodies. Higher concentrations could be an indication of organic pollution such as from domestic sewage, industrial waste and fertilizer run-off. Natural seasonal fluctuations also occur as a result of the death and decay of aquatic organisms, particularly phytoplankton and bacteria in nutritionally rich waters. Nitrogen and phosphorus are the major control factors for the propagation of algae.

3. The Death of a Water body

Eutrophication is a process in which bodies of water (lakes, ponds, and rivers) receive excess nutrients that stimulate excessive growth of algae. eutrophication describes the qualitative conditions of an aquatic environment that has been disrupted.

The two most common nutrients that initiate eutrophication are nitrogen and phosphorous, two limiting nutrients in the growth of algae. These Two nutrients are usually introduced to the body of water through fertilizer run-off. The society as a whole needs to be aware of the problem in terms of health, environment finance, and recreation as well as the costs related to its solution.

The main cause of eutrophication is the large input of nutrients to a water body and the main effect is the imbalance in the food web that results in high levels of phytoplankton biomass in stratified water bodies. This can lead to algal blooms. The uncontrolled growth of algae and their subsequent descent into the depths of the body of water stimulates an active benthic community (bacteria), which depletes oxygen levels due to respiration. The direct consequence is an excess of oxygen consumption near the bottom of the water body.

The algae may also cover the surface of the water, reducing the amount of light that decreasing photosynthesis. The decreased level of dissolved oxygen can result in the death of larger aquatic communities.

Eutrophication is when the environment becomes enriched with nutrients. This can be a problem in marine habitats such as lakes as it can cause algal blooms.

- Fertilisers are often used in farming, sometimes these fertilisers run-off into nearby water causing an increase in nutrient levels.
- This causes phytoplankton to grow and reproduce more rapidly, resulting in algal blooms.
- This bloom of algae disrupts normal ecosystem functioning and causes many problems.

- The algae may use up all the oxygen in the water, leaving none for other marine life. This results in the death of many aquatic organisms such as fish, which need the oxygen in the water to live.

- The bloom of algae may also block sunlight from photosynthetic marine plants under the water surface.

- Some algae even produce toxins that are harmful to higher forms of life. This can cause problems along the food chain and affect any animal that feeds on them.

4. Effect of eutrophication on Water resources and Society

In aquatic environments, enhanced growth of choking aquatic vegetation or phytoplankton i.e. algal bloom) disrupts normal functioning of the ecosystem, causing a variety of problems. Human society is impacted as well: eutrophication decreases the resource value of rivers, lakes, and estuaries such that recreation, fishing, hunting, and aesthetic enjoyment are hindered contains high concentrations of nitrates and phosphates, which led to the quick growth as well as death of plants and algae.

A number of agricultural process contribute to nutrient pollution and "dead zones" in freshwater and coastal ecosystems. Fertilizers are applied to crop fields at the wrong time in the growing season or in amounts that exceed crop needs, resulting in nutrient runoff to water bodies. The toxicity of Lake sites is therefore usually not of an acute, but of a chronic nature, as humans as well as aquatic life are typically exposed only to the low concentrations in water, which however can be maintained over a long period of time in the surroundings of a contaminated site also dependent on rainfall events. Factory farms raising livestock frequently poorly manage or improperly dispose of their manure, allowing it to leach into nearby water bodies.

A sudden increase in orthophosphate in Lake water stimulated great increases in the growth of algae, as well as other aquatic plants. Algal blooms can lead to depletion of the oxygen that is dissolved in the water. Phosphates level increased through the breakdown of organic debris and sewage. Low DO values indicating heavy contamination by organic matter due to increased value of BOD and COD indicated the high pollution load produce by waste matter. Higher level of eutrophication in Sagar Lake leads to decrease in DO value. Algal blooms potentially produce toxins and can lead to depletion of the oxygen that is dissolved in the water.

Greenish yellow Coloured water restricts the penetration of light, which subsequently retard the photosynthetic reactions. This also indirectly affects the reoxygenation capacity of receiving water. Warm waters are more susceptible to eutrophication a build-up of nutrients and possible algal blooms because photosynthesis and bacterial decomposition both work faster at higher temperatures. Algal blooms limit the sunlight available to bottom-dwelling organisms and cause wide swings in the amount of dissolved oxygen in the water. Nutrients can come from many sources, such as fertilizers applied to agricultural fields, domestic drainage, municipal sewage, deposition of nitrogen from the atmosphere and erosion of soil containing nutrients from nearby catchment area. Higher pH value indicated higher degree of eutrophication in Lake. The high value of chloride content an indication of organic pollution due to the disposal of industrial, sewage effluents, agricultural and road run-off. Higher Ammonia indicated organic pollution. This arising from the breakdown of nitrogenous organic and inorganic matter in Lakes water, excretion by biota, reduction of the nitrogen gas in water Eutrophication promotes excessive plant growth and decay, favors certain weedy species over others, and is likely to cause severe reductions in water quality. DO levels decline to hypoxic levels, fish and other marine animals suffocate. Finally this ecosystem experiences an increase in nutrients, species such as algae experience a population increase (algal bloom). Hence lake water cannot be much fit for drinking, irrigation and domestic used. The average of alkalinity has exceeded due to improper drainage system. It is recommended that lakes water analysis should be carried out from time to time to monitor the rate and kind of contamination.

The ratio of nitrogen to phosphorus compounds in a water body is an important factor determining which of the two elements will be the limiting factor, and consequently which one has to be controlled in order to reduce a bloom

5. Eutrophication and Water Quality

In eutrophied lakes and reservoirs when measures have been taken to improve water quality by reducing or removing nitrogen and/or phosphorus without effect, it is largely due to the enormous amounts of nutrients stored in sediments being constantly released into the water. This shows the need to avoid nutrient loading into the water bodies as early as possible by proper management and planning practices. In the case of severe biomass accumulation, the process of oxidation of the organic matter that has formed into sediment at the bottom of the water body will consume all the available oxygen. Even the oxygen contained in sulphates (SO_4^{2-}) will be used by specific bacteria. This will lead to the release of sulphur (S^{2-}) that will immediately capture the free oxygen still present in the upper layers. Thus, the water body will loose all its oxygen and all life will disappear. Still, it has often been difficult to reduce nutrient inputs of diffuse source such as drainage water and erosion from agriculture or dumping grounds; this cannot be collected for treatment, unlike point source pollution from industrial or municipal wastewater. Water is unique chemical, essential for human survival; its eutrophication is a matter of grave concern. About 80 per cent of India's diseases are caused by the use of eutrophicated water. Efforts to make important water bodies pollution-free should reduce the amount of waste in effluent water from industries by reutilizing or recycling their components. Point source pollution can be treated by environmental technology.

aquaculture operations discharge large amounts of nitrogen and phosphorus from uneaten food, excrements, and other organic waste into lakes and coastal areas.

All of these actions pollute waterways with too many nutrients like nitrogen and phosphorous. These nutrients spur toxic algae blooms that can destroy habitat, cause fish kills, alter aquatic ecosystems, and contribute to dead zones.

6. Controlling Pollution through Water Quality Management

Efforts to control agricultural pollution must be part of a larger, holistic water quality management strategy that provides the scientific basis for effective actions, regulatory requirements, and voluntary components where regulatory requirements are not possible or wise. Adequate data on the amounts and types of pollutants reaching surface waters and their impacts on water quality must be collected, followed by the application of reliable, predictive pollutant-loading and water-quality models. These models can be used to support the development of realistic water quality goals, develop and assess alternatives, and inform the selection of strategies to reduce pollutants. The water quality management strategy facilitates the adoption of environmental standards such as water quality standards and watershed pollutant loading caps and the implementation of programs to achieve them.

7. Sources of nutrients and eutrophication and nutrient enrichment

All activities in the entire drainage area of a lake or reservoir are reflected directly or indirectly in the water quality of these water bodies. A lake or reservoir may, however, be naturally eutrophied when situated in a fertile area with naturally nutrient enriched soils. In many lakes and reservoirs wastewater is the main source since untreated wastewater or wastewater treated only by a conventional mechanical- biological methods still contains nitrogen and phosphorus. Both nitrogen and phosphorus can be removed by well-known technology - phosphorus by addition of a chemical that precipitates phosphate though a chemical reaction, and nitrogen usually by biological means through micro- organism activity.

Drainage water from agricultural land also contains phosphorus and nitrogen. It usually has much more nitrogen because phosphorus is usually bound to soil components. Extensive use of fertilizers results in significant concentrations of nutrients particularly nitrogen, in agricultural runoff. If eroded soil reaches the lake, both phosphorus and the nitrogen in the soil contribute to eutrophication. Erosion is often caused by deforestation which also results from unwise planning and management of the resource.

Wetlands are increasingly used to solve the problem of diffuse pollution from agriculture which cause eutrophication. Nitrate is converted in wetlands to free nitrogen and released to the air. This is not harmful, as free nitrogen compromises about 4/5ths of the atmosphere. Phosphorus is adsorbed by wetland soils and, like nitrogen, is taken up by the plants. Both nitrogen and phosphorus may therefore be removed by wetlands. In addition, it is often also necessary to control fertilizer usage in agricultural practices as the majority may end up in the drainage area, if the diffuse pollution from nutrients is to be reduced sufficiently to improve water quality.

Rain water contains phosphorus and nitrogen from air pollution. As nitrogen is more mobile in the atmosphere than phosphorus, it is usually over 20 times more concentrated than phosphorus. Nitrogen can only be reduced in rain water by extensive controls of the air pollution in the entire region. One can safely say that the main sources of pollution in the atmosphere are from industries and automobile exhaust without proper filtering systems.

Nitrogen and phosphorus present in the excess food is dissolved or suspended in the water. The use of lakes for aquaculture therefore needs careful environmental planning and management practices by the owners and workers.

The sediment of a lake -its muddy bottom layer -contains relatively high concentrations of nitrogen and phosphorus. These can be released to water, particularly under conditions of low oxygen concentrations. The nutrients in the sediment come from the past settling of algae and dead organic matter. The nutrients released from sediments are referred to as the lake's internal loading.

It is possible but very expensive to remove the upper nutrient-rich layer of sediment. Covering sediments with clay to seal them and thereby reduce internal loading has also been tried. Even when nutrients are removed in large amounts from wastewater, agricultural drainage water and rain, it often takes much time before nutrient concentrations fall in the upper sediment layer because they are still present in the water environment. Early reduction or elimination of nutrient sources is therefore very important.

Chlorophyll a roughly indicates the concentration of plant biomass (on average 1% of algae biomass is chlorophyll a.

In a lake heavily loaded with wastewater, eutrophication is limited by nitrogen, as the nitrogen concentration in the discharged wastewater is only four times the phosphorus concentration. Such lakes often display extensive blooms of blue-green algae as unsightly surface scum. Some species of blue-green algae use nitrogen directly from the air and grow, although dissolved nitrogen is limiting. Lakes that receive natural tributaries and drainage water from agriculture, however, have high nitrogen concentrations and are therefore usually limited by phosphorus.

As phosphorus is more easily and less expensively removed from wastewater than nitrogen, in many cases (but not all) the best environmental management strategy for lakes and reservoirs is to remove as much phosphorus as possible from wastewater.

The appearance of certain algal blooms due to the eutriphied waters may bring the release of highly toxic substances in the water which in turn may cause liver and kidney damage or even death to cattle and humans. Eutrophication is a process which could be prevented by undertaken proper planning and management measurers within the watershed and the water bodies.

If eutrophication has already started it is very difficult and costly to control or revert. Around the world there are some eutrophied lakes, but the majority of the world's lakes are not. This situation is changing rapidly.

Waters in eutrophic lakes and reservoirs bring enormous losses of biodiversity, reduced water quality and availability. Furthermore, such lakes and reservoirs represent a significant health hazard for humans and animals alike. This is primarily due to the explosive growth of microscopic algae which once dead and in the process of decay release one of the most powerful classes of toxins known to man: Cyanotoxins. Damage to electric power plants and recreational activities are also well recorded as negative impacts originated from these process cause large economic losses.

To control the process of eutrophication there is a need to understand the causes and the stages of development. Similarly, it is necessary to carefully assess and evaluate the technological solutions to be applied in the mitigation and remediation of the eutrophication process. In general conventional wastewater treatment systems are sufficient for the purpose although they tend to be very expensive to maintain. Alternative methods of eutrophication control and mitigation include the use of natural wetlands as well as constructed ones since they are based on the capacity of self purification of nature and are usually much cheaper to maintain and operate.

Eutrophication exhibited our ignorance towards our lakes, reservoirs and rivers in many ways can be reflected the careless way in which society is dealing with its liquid wastes as well as the application of unsound land use practices. It is expected that through this publication citizens together with the authorities, industries, farmers and other members of the society can grasp the principles of this process, the effects and remediation so that proactive, co-operative action can be taken to prevent or significantly reduce the risk of surface water bodies becoming polluted through the process of eutrophication.

Eutrophication is one of the most widespread environmental problems of inland waters, and is their unnatural enrichment with two plant nutrients, phosphorus and nitrogen.

One important result of lake and reservoir enrichment is increased growth of microscopic floating plants, algae, and the formation of dense mats of larger floating plants. Growth results from the process of photosynthesis which is how the plants generate organic compounds and biomass through the uptake of nutrients (nitrogen, phosphorus and others) from the soil and water. In the process light acts as the energy source and carbon dioxide dissolved in water as the carbon source. As a result of the photosynthetic process oxygen is also produced. The nutrient level of many lakes and rivers has increased dramatically over the in response to increased discharge of domestic wastes and non-point pollution from agricultural practices and urban development. nutrient enrichment, especially phosphorus (P) and nitrogen (N), has been considered as a major threat to the health of coastal marine waters. Once a water body is eutrophicated, it will lose its primary functions and subsequently influence sustainable development of economy and society.

Algae display varying degrees of complexity depending on the organization of their cells. Macroalgae, phytoplankton and cyanobacteria may colonize marine, brackish or fresh waters wherever conditions of light, temperature and nutrients are favourable.

When the plants die they decompose due to bacterial and fungi activity; in the process oxygen is consumed and the nutrients are released together with carbon dioxide and energy. In many lakes and reservoirs in the world plants growing in the surface during spring and summer will die during autumn and sink to the bottom where they decompose.

During spring and summer, lakes and reservoirs are often supersaturated with oxygen due to the amount of plants. The oxygen surplus is released to the atmosphere and no longer available to decompose organic matter. This causes oxygen depletion in the deeper layers of lakes, particularly in autumn. Oxygen depletion is therefore caused by the shifts in time and space between photosynthesis and decomposition. In tropical areas the same process takes place, but seasonally speaking it is not as representative as in temperate areas because temperature and daylight duration is very similar throughout the year.

Oxygen depletion often leads to complete deoxygenation or anoxia in the deep layers of the lake or reservoirs also because oxygen poorly dissolves in water. In shallow lakes and where plant production is high, deoxygenation of the sediment and water occur frequently too. Such conditions kill fish and invertebrates. Moreover, ammonia and hydrogen sulfide originated from bacterial activity can be released from sediments under conditions of anoxia, and their concentrations can rise to levels which adversely affect plants and animals as they act as poisonous gases (also hydroelectrical power facilities in reservoirs often suffer because of the corrosive power of hydrogen sulfide). Phosphorus and ammonia may also be released into the water, further enriching it with nutrients.

Some particular type of algae, which grow in highly nutrient enriched lakes and reservoirs, release in the water very powerful toxins which are poisonous at very low concentrations. Some of the toxins produce negative effects on the liver of life stock at minimal concentrations but they can lead to the death of cattle and other animals even to humans when ingested in drinking water at higher concentrations. one way to treat and disinfect surface waters where these algae grow and to prevent high concentration of organic matter is to use chlorine, unfortunately this leads to the formation of compounds which may produce or induce cancer -a serious threat to the safety of drinking water supplies. High concentrations of nitrogen in the form of nitrate in water can also cause public health problems. They can inhibit the ability of infants to incorporate oxygen into their blood and so result in a condition called the blue baby syndrome or methemoglobinemia. For this to occur, nitrate levels must be above 10mg per liter in drinking water. The condition can be life-threatening.

One of the main problems occurring as a result of algal blooms or other aquatic plants (disproportionate growth) is the reduction in transparency in the water which reduces the recreational value of lakes, particularly for swimming and boating. Water hyacinth and Nile cabbage can cover large areas near the shore and can float into open water spreading at times over the entire surface. These mats can block light to submerged plants and produce large quantities of dead organic matter that can lead to low oxygen concentrations and the emission of unpleasant gases such as methane and hydrogen sulfide due to its decomposition or decay. Masses of these plants can restrict access for fishing or recreational uses of lakes and reservoirs and can block irrigation and navigation channels.

This results from the changes in the water and food quality together with decreased oxygen concentration which often alter the composition of the fish fauna from more to less desirable species. Nevertheless, yields of certain species of fish tend to increase as eutrophication increases since there is more food available. However, oxygen depletion and high ammonia concentrations under hypereutrophic conditions can lead to decreases in fish yields as eutrophication rises.

The demand for surface water for many purposes is increasing globally, mainly due to population growth and irrigation, particularly in arid and semi-arid regions. Eutrophication often becomes apparent to the public as populations increase in density. There is clear evidence that nutrient loading to lakes, estuaries and coastal oceans has greatly increased through human activities over the past few decades and that this has caused or enhanced many of the symptoms of the aquatic ecosystem transformation known as eutrophication. There are different opinions on the relationship of nutrient enrichment to water eutrophication and algal bloom: (1) When P concentration in water is low, it may be the limiting factor for inducing water eutrophication and algal bloom; (2) When P concentration in water increases rapidly, other may become a new limiting factor, such as pH, water depth, temperature, light, wave, wind or other biological factors; (3) The influence of N and P still lasts for a longer time because of the high development level of our society.

8. Different aspects of Eutrophication

Water eutrophication is one of the most challenging environmental problems in the world. The increasing severity of water eutrophication has been brought to the attention of both the governments and the public in recent years. The mechanisms of water eutrophication are not fully understood, but excessive nutrient loading into surface water system is considered to be one of the major factors. Water resources are environmental assets and therefore have a price. There are market-based methods to estimate costs and benefits, and these make as a useful tool to assess the economic effects of abatement of eutrophication and other pollution problems. Benefits range from higher quality drinking water and reduced health risks to improved recreational uses. The effects on human health from the lack of sanitation and the chronic effects of toxic algal blooms are two of the many indirect effects resulting from eutrophication. Numerous cost-benefit analyses of pollution abatement have clearly demonstrated that the total costs to society of 'no pollution reduction' is much higher than at least a 'reasonable pollution reduction'.

Several management strategies were developed and applied to solve problems of decreasing surface and groundwater quality. These were often a response to acute critical situations resulting in increased costs of water. The demand for good quality fresh water was only solved partially and locally; this was because too few resources were allocated too late to solve the problems.

The need to integrate social and cultural issues in a new management strategy. A new management approach is needed which integrates scientific and technological knowledge with social, cultural and political issues for sustainable development of water resources for human needs. The implementation of the watershed concept by establishing national and international Watershed Committees is fundamental in developing effective management strategies for lakes and reservoirs. Based on the ecosystem concept and an integrated planning approach, the training of decision-makers and managers is an indispensable component in this strategy.

It is often not safe to consume water in developing countries. Changes to perceptions of the value of water to meet changes in the management of water resources, the need of the aquatic environment and the entire ecosystems in these countries are needed. It will be difficult to make such changes given current inertia towards the value of water, but public awareness and environmental education are steps in the right direction.

Many factors affect water quality in developing countries, particularly increasing eutrophication: industrialization, urban development, new land-use practices and change in the use of water. Given these changes, it is important to integrate hydrological, social, economic and cultural aspects with scientifically-based knowledge of lakes and reservoirs. The social aspects of eutrophication are often overwhelming in developing countries. The loss of jobs resulting from heavy fish kills due to oxygen depletion is just one example of a massive social impact resulting from eutrophication.

A new management strategy should recommend several alternatives to present practices. For instance, one should recommend that soil erosion can be stopped or at least reduced by stopping deforestation and burning techniques in farming. Implementing prevention, control and management of eutrophication within an integrated strategy can provide new job opportunities and tools for economic development, with corresponding social benefits.

The restoration of polluted lakes is another activity that is increasingly used in industrialized countries. For effective lake management, restoration, however, has to work hand in hand with the removal of nutrient sources to treat both causes and symptoms.

Pollution abatement is expensive, particularly when it involves advanced environmental technology to significantly reduce nutrient loadings. This is the cost of an increased population density, urbanization and production.

Massive urbanization always makes it more difficult to solve water-quality problems afterwards, whereas a proper allocation of activities in the entire drainage area facilitates a more cost-effective solution. Therefore solution of water eutrophication and recovery of the multiple functions of the water system have become the key issues for environmental biologists.

Assessment of water eutrophication

There are many different assessment parameters, the concentrations of total nitrogen and phosphorus are the two basic ones. Physical and chemical evaluation parameters were used to assess water eutrophication, mainly nutrient concentration (N and P), algal chlorophyll, water transparency and dissolved oxygen. Relation of chlorophyll a to other parameters.

The available parameters concerned include total nitrogen (TN), total phosphorus (TP), dissolved oxygen (DO), chemical oxygen demand by K_2MnO_4 oxidation method (COD_{Mn}), biological oxygen demand (BOD_5), etc., various eutrophicated water. Eutrophication or red tide occurs when N concentration in water reaches 300 $\mu g/L$ and P concentration reaches 20 $\mu g/L$.

harmfulness of water eutrophication is that it can break out the intrinsic equilibrium of the aquatic ecosystem and lead to the damage of the water ecosystem and the gradual degeneration of its functions. It can affect water quality and make transparency of water become worse than ever. Thus, little sunlight can penetrate water body and photosynthesis of plants under the water will be weakened or even stopped. Water eutrophication can also cause the super saturation or lack of dissolved oxygen in water, which will be dangerous to aquatic animals and cause great death to them. Eutrophic systems tend to accumulate large amounts of organic carbon causing a shift in organic matter biochemical composition. Meanwhile, because of water eutrophication, a mass of algae, mainly Cyanophyta and green algae, bloom and form a thick layer of "green scum" on water surface. Algae can release toxins and render the organic matters in water to be decomposed into harmful gases, which will poison the fish and seashell.

The harmfulness of eutrophication also includes causing the shortage supply of drinking water source by degrading water quality. When the blooming algae die, they can produce lots of algae's toxin which is harmful to human health. apart from. Besides, increased nitrite concentration in the eutrophic water will be dangerous to human health, too, as products of nitrite nitrification process is a strong carcinogen. Thus, the exacerbation of water eutrophication with the increased severity of algae blooming in surface water system has attracted great attention of both public and private sections.

9. Eutrophication abatement and Awareness

Eutrophication abatement can be success by strong public support of citizens and stake-holders combined with effective legislative measures and monitoring programs. The best results were obtained when control measures began early and long before hyper-eutrophication occurred. problems involving point sources were relatively easily solved, while those involving non-point sources were more difficult to resolve. The environmental strategy indicated cannot be realized only with a large amount of financial resources, but also through proper environmental education and understanding at all levels, from undergraduate schools to universities, and from decision-makers to all citizens.

These programs are crucial to both agricultural productivity and environmental protection. Technical assistance programs must keep pace with intensifying agricultural production in their scope and availability.

Reduction of non-point pollution in areas with extensive agriculture requires the construction of wetlands as a buffer between fields and rivers and lakes.

In every country of the world has government programs to assist farmers. Technical assistance can include expert guidance on practices like incorporating conservation methods to improve water management, protecting water quality, controlling erosion, managing manure, properly and effectively using fertilizers, transitioning to organic farming, and applying new technologies. It is essential to provide funding to farmers to engage in conservation practices, like converting marginal or erodible lands to forests or grasslands, planting grass or forest buffers along streams to trap pollutants, protecting habitats, planting cover crops, or building fences to keep livestock out of streams. Humans need water as much as food. So the need to feed a growing global population cannot be allowed to impair our ever-scarcer water resources. Using less detergents and detergents with no or little polyphosphates can reduce phosphorus loads considerably.

Nor does it have to. It is mandatory to encourage management techniques, policies, and regulations to reduce agriculture's impact on water—and new tools continue to be developed. We just need the resources and will to implement them.

Increased nutrient load to water body is now recognized as a major threat to the structure and functions of near shore coastal ecosystems, and severe eutrophication problems associated with harmful algal bloom is a major manifestation. Although related to nutrient enrichment in general, the basic cause of water eutrophication is more connected to an imbalance in the load of nitrogen and phosphorus with respect to silica.

Urbanization, industrialization and agricultural practices, have threatened the inland fresh water reservoirs with effluents. The indiscriminate dumping of municipal sewage into these ecosystems have added to the eutrophication problem which is now the central concern of water pollution control.

The problem of water eutrophication has become more and more severe worldwide, but the mechanism of its occurrence has not been fully understood. The limited knowledge of water eutrophication processes will add difficulties for the prevention and remediation of water eutrophication. Therefore, more researches should be turned to the mechanisms of water eutrophication under different watershed conditions.

The degree of eutrophication is determined by the number of harmful algal blooms: a bloom containing 0.5 to 1 million cells per litre or by the oxygen concentration in the lower depth of the lakes.

The organic waste effects productivity and the composition of aquatic life, increasing the biomass. The increase in nutrients results in more rapid growth and even in the growth of fish. The more serious result is the increase in algal mass and macrophytic vegetation and induces fish kills. Filters of water treatment plants also get clogged and undesirable taste and odours result leading to increased cost of operation.

Much of the nutrients entering the lake are incorporated into algae, which release the nutrients back into water either alive or dead. Some algal blooms release toxic substances that kill fish, domestic animals and birds and the water begins to stink. Blooms also damage the recreational lakes by interfering with fishing, bathing, boating and often reduce the beauty of the lake.

Lake eutrophication can be controlled or its effects minimised by increasing the nutrients and controlling excessive algae growth in lakes. The algal blooms can be removed by harvesting and mechanical removal processes.

Nutrients such as phosphorus and nitrogen compounds can be removed through precipitations and physic-chemical methods. Chemicals like copper sulphate, sodium arsenite and zirconium oxychloride can also check algal blooming. Nitrogen can be removed by biological nitrification, denitrification and air stripping of ammonia from alkalized waste water.

Control of water bodies and of organisms which protect water should be reinforced by all available means including legal enforcement. A beginning should be made with effective sewage disposal in urban areas.

Active participation by citizens in abating eutrophication is impossible without their understanding of the problem. This requires environmental education of citizens. how to introduce environmental education and to increase public awareness. In many industrialized countries, a number of leaflets and booklets on environmental information are distributed free to the public. environmental education as follows: Environmental education is a permanent process in which individuals gain awareness of their environment and acquire the knowledge, values, skills, experiences and also the determination which enable them to act individually and collectively to solve present and future environmental problems. It is therefore a continuous, lifelong process.

ABOUT THE AUTHOR

Dr. Hemant Pathak held positions as Assistant Professor in the department of chemistry, Govt. Indira Gandhi Engineering College, Sagar, MP, India. He had extensive experience in teaching, research and administrative management.

Dr. Pathak received his Ph.D. degree in chemistry from Dr. Hari Singh Gour Central University, Sagar, India and M.Sc. Gold medalist from Jiwaji University, Gwalior. He has published 07 books and more than 50 research papers in reputed International and National journals and received several awards. He is a member of editorial boards and reviewer boards of several international journals and societies. His area of specialization includes Engineering Chemistry and Environmental Pollution management.

www.ingramcontent.com/pod-product-compliance
Lightning Source LLC
Chambersburg PA
CBHW080809290526
45790CB00008B/3638

*9 7 8 1 4 8 4 1 7 1 4 2 4 *